MW00638517

MEANGIRLS

YOU'RE SO **FETCH**

RP **STUDIO**

PHILADELPHIA

You love

---

as much as Gretchen loves plaid.

That time you

_____

was so fetch.

WINTER TALENT SHOW

If you were performing for the
Winter Talent Show, you would sing

_____

You taught me that being a real friend means

_____

You're such a Janis when you

_____

Cady makes it to the Mathletes State Championship. If you were to qualify for a championship it would be for

_____

You were such a regulation hottie when

_____

What I most admire about you is

_____

The North Shore student you're most likely
to hang out with is

_____

QUEEN BEE

If Regina George is flawless, then

that would make you

_____

You deserve all the candy cane grams
in the world because

_____

Kevin Gnapoor's business card says

MATH ENTHUSIAST/BAD-ASS M.C.

Your business card would say

_____

Like Gretchen's white gold hoops or Regina's "R" pendant, your most prized possession is your

_____

I'll never forget that time we

_____

Your greatest qualities are

_____

and

_____

Like Kälteen bars,

---

with you is never a good idea.

We make a great duo when

_____

I'd choose you for

Spring Fling Queen because

_____

If I baked you a cake filled with rainbows
and smiles, it would be because

_____

My favorite thing about you is

_____

Janis's calling might be moderately priced soaps, but your calling is

_____

I'M A MOUSE, DUH!

If you were invited to Chris Eisel's Halloween party, the costume you'd most likely wear is

_____

It was so "grool" when you

_____

Cady Heron looks good in army pants and flip-flops, but your go-to outfit is

_____

Regina George may be teen royalty, but she'll never have anything on your

_____

Janis and Damian wear matching purple tuxedos to the Spring Fling. If we wore matching outfits, it would probably be

_____

A LITTLE
BIT
DRAMATIC

Regina wears a shirt that says,

A LITTLE BIT DRAMATIC.

If you had a shirt with your slogan,

it would say

_____

The best thing about our friendship is

_____

Cady may be amazing at calculus, but
you've always been the best at

_____

Regina thinks Janis's dream is to dive into a big pile of girls, but your dream come true is

_____

Cady lived in Africa for twelve years.
If you lived somewhere that long,
it would probably be

_____

You are happiest when

_____

If you were in a social clique at
North Shore High, it would be

_____

Just like Cady, you're the
perfect combination of

_____

and

_____

Kevin Gnapoor is the captain of the Mathletes club. If you were the captain of a club, it would be

_____

Thanks for thinking of me when

_____

On Wednesdays the Plastics wear pink.

You look your best when

_____

Gretchen Wieners can't help it that she's popular, just like you can't help that you're

_____

You showed me that you're the lion and not the warthog when you

_____

Karen's special talent is sticking her whole fist in her mouth. Yours is

_____

I knew we'd be the best of friends when

_____

If you were in the Plastics,
you'd be known for your

_____

You have always had the best taste in

_____

You're like Karen when you

_____

Cady's math skills have nothing on your

_____

I'm so thankful we're friends because

_____

You're so fetch.

RP Studio™
Hachette Book Group
1290 Avenue of the Americas, New York, NY 10104
www.runningpress.com
@Running_Press

First Edition: September 2024

Published by RP Studio, an imprint of Hachette Book Group, Inc. The RP Studio name and logo are trademarks of Hachette Book Group, Inc.

Running Press books may be purchased in bulk for business, educational, or promotional use. For more information, please contact your local bookseller or the Hachette Book Group Special Markets Department at Special.Markets@hbgusa.com.

The publisher is not responsible for websites (or their content) that are not owned by the publisher.

Design by Jackie Schlindwein

ISBN: 978-0-7624-8708-0

Printed in China

APS

10 9 8 7 6 5 4 3 2 1